LIVING FOSSILS

Platypuses

Caitie McAneney

PowerKiDS press.
New York

Published in 2015 by The Rosen Publishing Group, Inc.
29 East 21st Street, New York, NY 10010

First Edition

Editor: Sarah Machajewski
Book Design: Mickey Harmon

Photo Credits: Cover, pp. 1–24 (border texture) Markus Gann/Shutterstock.com; cover (logo texture), pp. 1–3, 4, 6, 8, 10, 12, 14, 16, 18–20, 22–24 (background texture) Bplanet/Shutterstock.com; cover (forward-facing platypus), p. 15 Jason Edwards/National Geographic/Getty Images; cover (sideways platypus), p. 22 worldswildlifewonders/Shutterstock.com; p. 5 (platypus) Theo Allofs/The Image Bank/Getty Images; p. 5 (echidna) Kristian Bell/Shutterstock.com; p. 7 Martin Harvey/Gallo Images/Getty Images; p. 9 (platypus swimming) Robin Smith/Photographer's Choice/Getty Images; p. 9 (spur) Jason Edwards/© National Geographic Image Collection/Alamy; p. 11 Auscape / UIG/Universal Images Group/Getty Images; p. 17 Bildagentur Zoonar GmbH/ Shutterstock.com; p. 18 (platypus) Joel Bauchat Grant/Shutterstock.com; p. 18 (koala) rickyd/Shutterstock.com; p. 18 (tiger) Denise Allison Coyle/Shutterstock.com; p. 19 http://commons.wikimedia.org/wiki/Platypus#mediaviewer/File:Platypus_skeleton_pengo.jpg; p. 21 Kletr/Shutterstock.com.

Library of Congress Cataloging-in-Publication Data

McAneney, Caitlin, author.
Platypuses / Caitie McAneney.
pages cm. — (Living fossils)
Includes bibliographical references and index.
ISBN 978-1-4777-5835-9 (pbk.)
ISBN 978-1-4777-5833-5 (6 pack)
ISBN 978-1-4777-5839-7 (library binding)
1. Platypus—Juvenile literature. 2. Rare mammals—Juvenile literature. 3. Living fossils—Juvenile literature. I. Title.
QL737.M72M34 2015
599.2'9—dc23
2014028987

Manufactured in the United States of America

CPSIA Compliance Information: Batch #CW15PK: For Further Information contact Rosen Publishing, New York, New York at 1-800-237-9932

Contents

Living Fossils

What animal has the tail of a beaver, body of an otter, bill of a duck, and lays eggs like a lizard? It's the platypus, a **species** that's outlived even the dinosaurs!

The platypus is part of the **mammal** family called Ornithorhynchidae (ohr-nih-thuh-RIHN-kih-dee). Some scientists believe this family split from other mammals around 166 million years ago. Platypuses are considered living **fossils**. Living fossils are animals that haven't changed much over millions of years, even when the rest of the species in their animal family have died out.

FOSSIL FACTS

The first time scientists saw a platypus, they thought it was fake! It didn't seem like an animal that could actually exist.

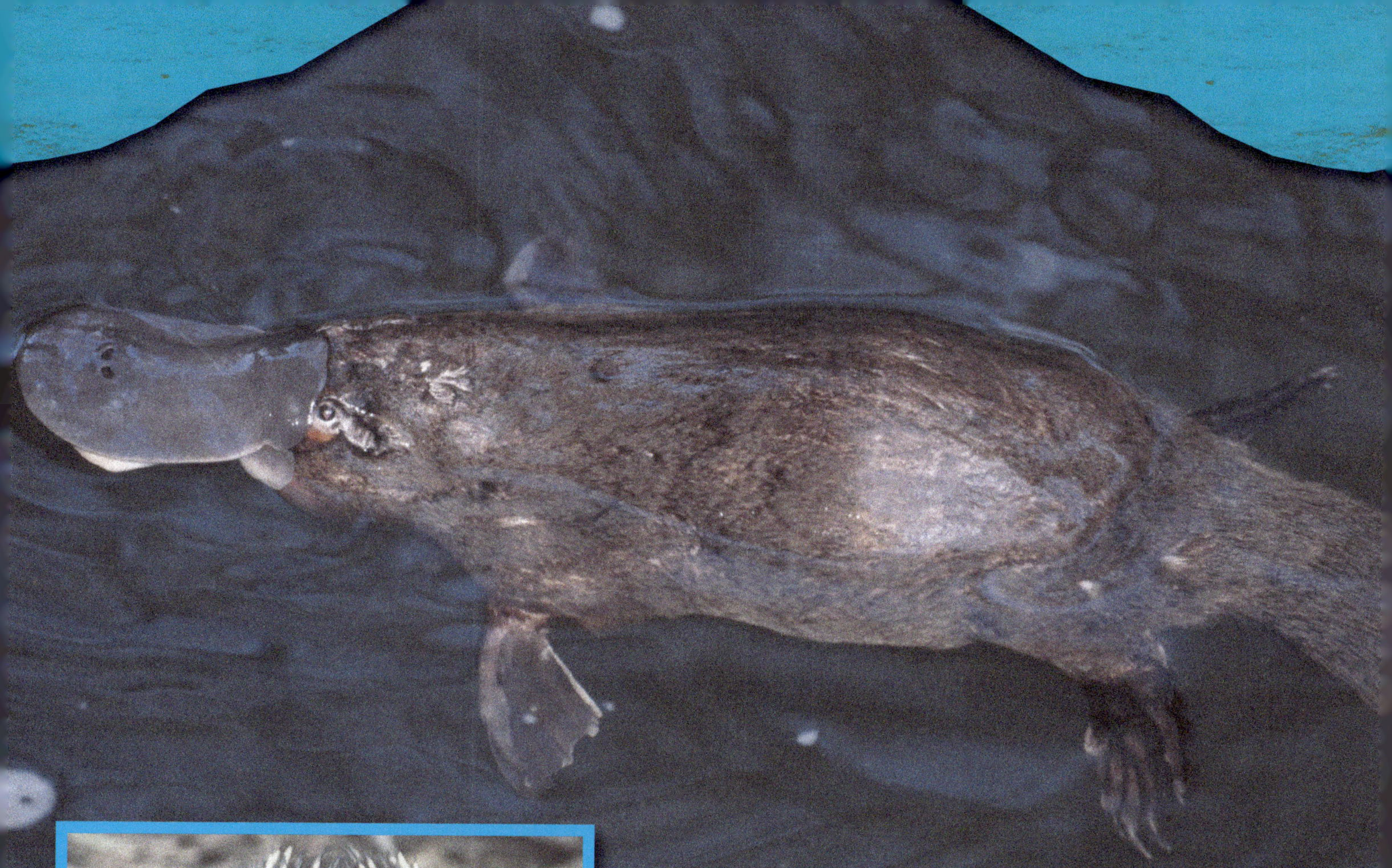

echidna

A monotreme is a mammal that lays eggs. Besides platypuses, the only other monotremes are echidnas.

Freshwater Habitats

Australia is home to many animals found nowhere else in the world. This includes the platypus, which lives in eastern Australia's freshwater **habitats**. Platypuses live in all kinds of freshwater, from warm rain forest rivers to cold mountain streams.

Platypuses are amphibious, which means they spend time both in water and on land. Their webbed feet make them great swimmers, so most of their time is spent in water. They build earthen dens, called burrows, near water. They fill their burrows with logs, sticks, and plants.

While platypuses make burrows on land, they'd rather be in the water. Their short legs make running a lot harder than swimming.

Freaky Features

The platypus may look like it was made from the parts of different animals. However, each part has a purpose, and each has helped the platypus survive for millions of years.

The platypus's webbed feet help it swim. Its tail helps it swim, too, but it also stores fat that can be used when there's not a lot of food. A platypus's fur is waterproof, which keeps it warm and dry. Male platypuses have a body part that's used for **defense**. It's a sharp spike on their heels, called a spur. It has strong **venom** inside!

FOSSIL FACTS

Platypus venom can kill small animals. If a platypus stings a person, it won't kill them. However, it causes terrible pain that can last for weeks.

Platypuses can retract, or pull back, the webbing on their feet so nails can come out. This helps them dig burrows and run on land.

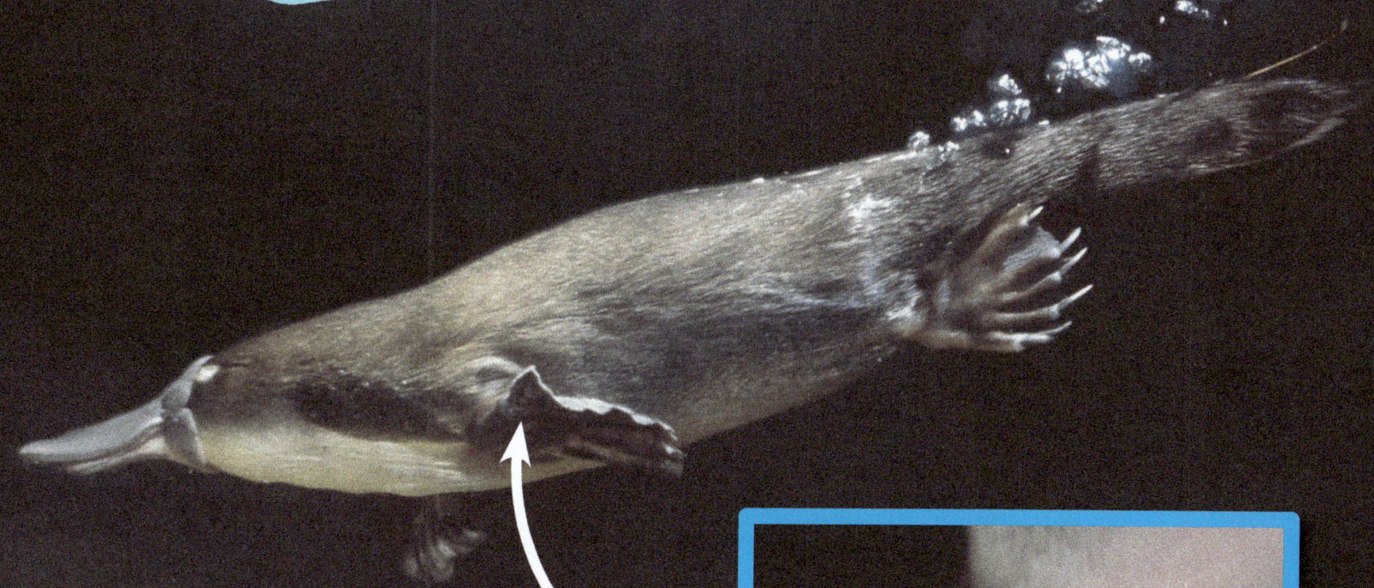

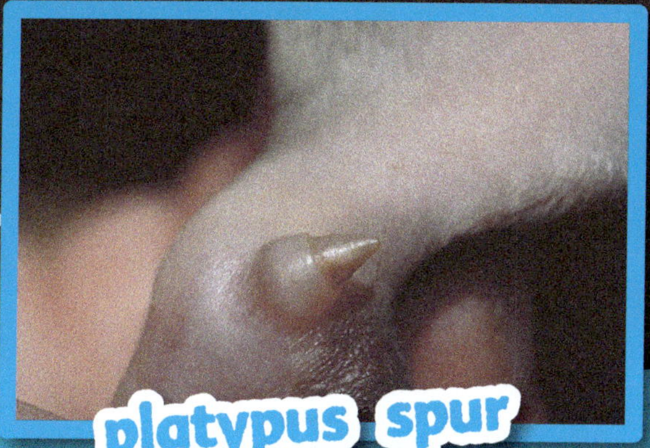

platypus spur

Platypus Superpower

You might see a platypus and think, "Is that bill necessary?" The answer is yes—it's actually their most useful part! It may be one of the reasons why the platypus species has lasted this long.

When platypuses swim, they keep their eyes and ears closed to keep out water. Their bill helps them sense where they are. Platypus bills have **receptors** on them. The receptors sense the movements of other animals. This is called electrolocation, and it helps platypuses locate their **prey**. Platypus prey includes shrimp, tadpoles, worms, snails, and sometimes flying bugs.

FOSSIL FACTS

Platypuses store the food they find in their cheeks. They eat it later, when they're above water and resting.

Platypuses hunt by swimming along the bottom of a body of water, searching for prey. This is called foraging.

A Day in the Life

A day in the life of a platypus can explain how it has survived for so long. First, it's nocturnal, or most active at night. Nocturnal animals can avoid being eaten by animals that travel through their habitats during the day. Also, platypuses don't spend very much time together. They can forage and hide better when they're alone.

A platypus spends most of its time in the water. Like an otter, a platypus's body is built for diving and swimming along riverbeds for food. A platypus can swim a little over three feet (0.9 m) per second. It can stay underwater for over two minutes!

This drawing shows what a platypus burrow looks like. Platypuses can hide there to stay safe.

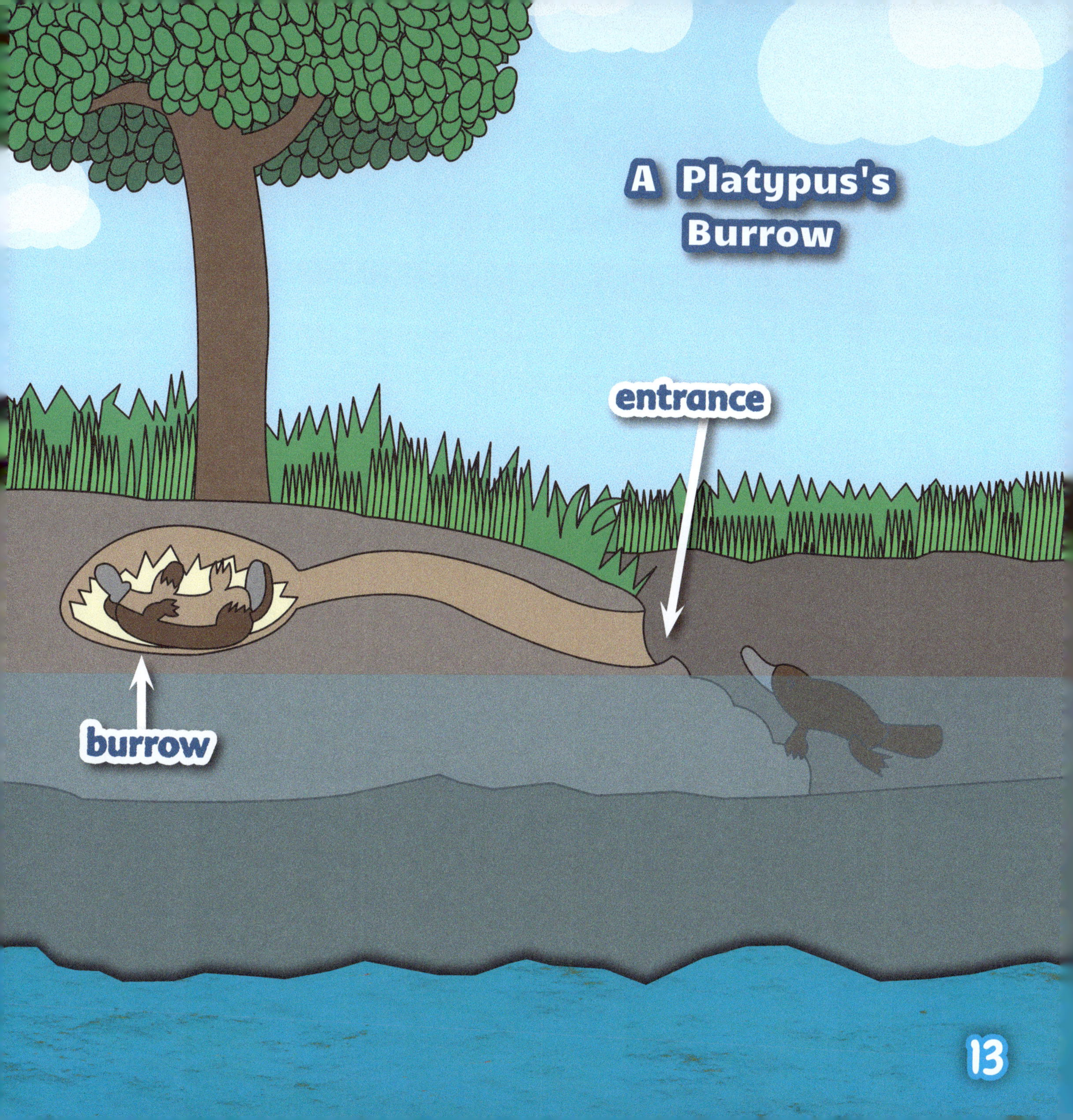
A Platypus's
Burrow
entrance
burrow

Making More Platypuses

Platypuses like to be alone, but they come together during **mating** season. Males fight for the females' attention. Sometimes, these fights get bloody. Males use their spurs to jab other males with venom. The winner gets the female.

After mating, the male and female part ways, and the female builds a large burrow. The female lays two to four eggs. She uses her tail to keep the eggs close to her body. When baby platypuses **hatch**, they're blind and have no fur. The mother feeds her babies milk.

FOSSIL FACTS

Baby platypuses are only the size of a lima bean when they hatch! They aren't able to go out on their own until they're about four months old.

Reptiles lay eggs. Mammals feed milk to their young. Platypuses do both!

Platypus Predators

The platypus is so good at hiding and spending its nights underwater that scientists aren't sure who its natural predators are. They think foxes and dingoes might hunt them on land. Crocodiles and pythons might hunt them in the water.

The platypus has defenses to help it survive attacks. These defenses include swimming fast and using their heel spurs. They can also use electrolocation to tell if a big animal is coming near. The platypus's biggest **threat** is a certain kind of **fungus**. It hurts the animal's skin and other parts of its body.

Unfortunately for the platypus, there's a special kind of tick that likes to feed on its skin. It only feeds on platypuses!

Fossil Clues

Just how long have platypuses survived? Scientists used to think the platypus became its own species between 17 and 65 million years ago. However, in 2007, they found a fossil that might give a better answer as to how long the platypus has been around.

These animals are all mammals, but they belong to different groups. Platypuses are only one of two animals in their group.

platypus skeleton

The fossil told scientists that the platypus may have been around for over 112 million years! While scientists aren't sure why platypuses have survived, they can point to how they've survived. Their bill, swimmer's body, and nocturnal behavior are all great defenses.

Harming Habitats

Platypuses have survived longer than the dinosaurs. However, there's one species that has the power to wipe them out—humans. Right now, platypuses are not in danger of becoming **extinct**. There are laws to keep them safe from hunters and people who want to catch them.

The greatest threat to platypuses is people ruining their habitat. These animals are built to live only in freshwater. When humans build on or near freshwater habitats, platypuses lose their homes. Also, pollution of the freshwater habitats of Australia can hurt platypuses and the animals they eat.

Much of Australia is still wild, which makes it a great habitat for animals. However, as more people build, animals' natural habitats become smaller.

Saving the Species

What if these living fossils survived for millions of years, just to become extinct because of humans? That would be terrible! Luckily, people have the power to save platypuses. We can follow laws to make sure they stay safe from hunters. We can also make sure their habitats aren't harmed.

Platypus populations aren't in danger right now. That's great news, because it means this species is still healthy. It also means that scientists have the opportunity to study these living fossils for years to come.

Glossary

defense: The act of protecting oneself. Also, something used to protect oneself.

extinct: No longer in existence.

fossil: Hardened remains of a plant or animal that lived long ago.

fungus: A living thing that is somewhat like a plant, but doesn't make its own food, have leaves, or have a green color. Fungi include molds and mushrooms.

habitat: An animal, plant, or other organism's natural home.

hatch: To break out of an egg.

mammal: A warm-blooded animal that has a backbone and hair, breathes air, and feeds milk to its young.

mate: To come together to make babies.

prey: An animal that is hunted by other animals for food.

receptor: A body part that responds to signals in the environment and carries the message back to the brain.

species: A group of plants or animals that are all the same kind.

threat: Something likely to cause harm.

venom: Something an animal makes in its body that can harm other animals.

Index

Websites

Due to the changing nature of Internet links, PowerKids Press has developed an online list of websites related to the subject of this book. This site is updated regularly. Please use this link to access the list: www.powerkidslinks.com/fos/plat